HAVE YOU FELT HIS TOUCH?

Then Give Him Praise

2nd Edition

Ronnie Fletcher

 www.trafford.com

North America & international
toll-free: 1 888 232 4444 (USA & Canada)
fax: 812 355 4082

Acknowledgements

I want to personally thank Bishop Carlton Brown for his support. I want to acknowledge his continuing effort to encourage me with my walk with the Lord. I want to give praise to the welcome mat his church has shown to me and everyone who enters the Lord's house in Harlem. May the Lord continue to bless him and his staff!

Thank You Again,

Ronnie Fletcher

Table of Contents

Thank You

It was a cloudy day as the church did fill.

When the Lord spoke in the month of April

The people gathered from near and far

Some came by train some came by car

He spoke to many, yet He was heard by few

Why He asked, do so many refuse to say thank you

People don't realize how lucky they are

Until they have a loved one knocking at my door

With so much to live for, I only ask for two

So why my children, is it so hard to say thank you?

Each morning you rise, is a blessing from Me

Just like when you close your eyes you trust in Thee

I've never promised you another day

Yet you go to sleep forgetting to pray

All have their moments and call my name

Only in fear or when they need someone to blame

So tonight when you lay down and have a moment or two

Remember My question, did you say thank you?

I Heard a Voice

While asleep, I saw a flash of light
Startled yet brave, I remained asleep last night
All of a sudden, it came without warning
It was a stranger's voice, who spoke without belonging
-Listen My Son-
Now I was awake as I trembled with fear
The voice then spoke, it's my cross you wear
I raised my head to face this bright light
The voice then spoke, everything's alright
-Listen My Son-
There have been many times you've required my hand
No matter your problem, I had to understand
Now you, my son, come walk with me
As the light grew bright, I knew it was Thee
-Yes My Lord-
Everyone on Earth has a reason, you see
But you may so, have a special gift from me
Many people in life, spend their whole time wishing
But you, my son, have been given a mission
-Yes My Lord-
This task I give you will be so clear
It will take your trust in me to show no fear
Walk through life with your head held high
When people question your smile, tell them it comes from the sky
-Yes My Lord-
The fire I give you will stay in your heart
But your mission in life will be difficult to start
So gather your strength, gather your pride
Because you now walk proud with the lord by your side
-Yes My Lord-

Today He Forgave Me

Today the question was loudly asked
Yet few could answer, few knew their task
Today the Bishop questioned our faith in Thee
Can the truth be told by you and me?
We bowed our heads to shed a tear
Do we pay attention, is it the Lord we hear?
We walk around, without knowing our fate
As we walk through life carrying burdens of weight
The Lord told us to trust in Thee
Yet we continue to question, how could this be?
The Lord gave Himself as His only son
Yet we continue to sin, and question the Holy One
The Lord gave instructions to be followed by man
Yet we question his way, because we don't understand
I sat and prayed to acknowledge my imperfection
Today I asked the Lord to give me direction
I trust my soul with the Holy Spirit of Thee
Please, my Father, save a wretch like me
The heavens opened, thunder sounded so loud
Yet when I looked up, there wasn't a cloud
I heard a voice, it said I forgive you my son
You have given your soul to the Holy One
Those who question you, those who ask why
Smile upon them and point to the sky

Tears of Thee

Tonight I had a visit from the Holy Spirit
Not one of you could see, but yes I could feel it
I sat down tonight with a heavy heart
It was the chill of the Spirit from the very start
Although I didn't understand, my eyes filled with tears
There was a feeling of the Lord that took away my fears
I closed my eyes and felt a moment and a chill
As the moment became intense, I knew it was God's will
I didn't know why my eyes filled with tears
The Spirit then embraced me, it was the Lord I could hear
Go out into the world, and please don't question why
Let people see Me, as they look into your eyes
Stand strong and proud because you have My Spirit
Only the non believers won't even understand it
They will knock you down, try to curse your word
It will be up to you to spread what you've heard
You, my son, have been chosen to write what you hear
Soon you will understand why your eyes shed My tears

Resurrection of Thee

The cross is a symbol of Jesus' last place on Earth

When He lived, people didn't value His worth

Jesus' words have been written as part of our history

Yet the symbol of the cross remains a symbol of the Lord's victory

He gave His life, He asked that we be forgiven

So we live in this world with the hope to keep living

As we come to the Lord's house to learn of His way

We learn Jesus' last words, He drew strength to say

Forgive them Lord, because they know not what they do

He gave His blood for the life of me and you

So if God's son can give His life for us

The last thing we should do is lose His trust

Each Sunday we learn of stories of our Lord

To los e faith in Jesus is something we can't afford

We give thanks to our Savior because our spirits are free

As we celebrate Easter and the Resurrection of Thee

Devil's Hangout

Come on people, listen to my word
My elders, like yours, all sounded absurd
Let's hang out tonight and party until dawn
Come to my hangout, where all my kind belong
We all had elders who talked until they were blue
After years of trying, they'll still love you
Come with my boys, come hang with my girls
Parents, teachers tell you of a whole different world
We all have dreams, we all have someone to blame
Yet in my hangout, it's always the same
There's just one rule that no one can break
It's a club for all, and the club's not fake
We don't ask questions, the decision is yours
Once you enter my hangout, there are no chores
You can see the place I call my hangout
It's seen every day, and it leaves no doubt
Full to capacity, yet people still come in
Little do they know, I am not their friend
So come to my hangout, don't listen to the rules
My hangout is a cemetery, which welcomes all fools

Praise Him

I came to this service to hear God's word
Listen to the Spirit, now that seemed absurd
So I looked around to witness who couldn't hear it
What I saw was people feeling the Holy Spirit
Now we go through life planning our days
So why do we forget to give the Lord His praise?
We all seem to forget how we beg Him to forgive
Yet do we listen to His voice when He directs how we live?
We live in a magical world of make believe
Hiding our flaws, creating deceit up our sleeves
The Lord created us in His own vision of sight
So why do we try to change what He considered right?
Instead of accepting our flaws and still giving Him praise
We wish and believe for our own magical days
If we would just accept what God has for us
There would be no problems, if we could only trust
But we all go through life wanting only to win
Did you make the same effort to just praise Him?

A Miracle on The Freeway

When you woke up, did you give God praise?

As we go through life expecting normal days

A stranger spoke of going to work expecting a regular day

But what he experienced instead, was a miracle on the freeway

He spoke of a car in front of his that spun out of control

As he hit the brakes, he saw his life unfold

He saw cars and trucks which had all lost control of how to drive

While driving to work, he didn't know if he would survive

He spoke of a truck splitting a car in two

While his car went into a spin, he didn't know what to do

He spoke of the car in his rear approaching too fast

With panic in his heart, he thought "how could I last?"

He didn't realize what was about to unfold

He had the Lord at the wheel, and in full control

As he walked from this multiple car accident, without any pain

Shook up by fright, he suddenly felt a sense of relief from his gain

He came to God's house to give the Lord praise

Removed of any doubts, he witnessed the miracle that day

With tears in his eyes, we listened to his evidence of the Lord's grace

He told of his blessing with tears streaming down his face

We listened to this man's break down of his day

As he recounted his miracle on the freeway

Angel in the Beauty Shop

One day while at work in a beauty shop
This woman spoke of how her day wouldn't stop
She spoke of how she had an elderly customer in her chair
As the woman spoke, she didn't seem to care
The stranger asked her, what seems to trouble her mind
As the hairdresser worked, she felt she had to be kind
But what the lady didn't know, was that she really didn't care
The stranger in the chair told her, your thoughts are unfair
The hairdresser thought to herself, I want to smoke
She was having a bad day, as she started to choke
The stranger in the chair stated, honey please don't
If you go outside for that cigarette, a child you won't
So the lady went outside, but she remembered the stranger's word
Unable to forget, she gave heed to what she heard
She went back inside to find her chair empty
The hairdresser became frantic, asking where is the lady?
Her co-workers asked her, who do you mean?
They all seemed puzzled as they questioned her to extremes
She said the old lady who sat in my chair
Where did she go, I went on my break for some air
Her co-workers told her, you never had a customer today
As she stared in disbelief, what did you say?
Her co-workers went in the back to get the video
And to her surprise, there wasn't anyone to show
The tape showed her talking to herself
Her hands doing hair, yet no-one but herself
If she didn't listen to the Angel she would've lost her way
Today she speaks of how an Angel visited the beauty shop that day

Give Up Something

On this cold Sunday, we met a new teacher

This powerful woman was the wife of our preacher

She spoke of the Lord, she gave no slack

As her voice rose, her spirit said "Give Back"

We experience God's anger through earthquakes and floods

Yet the Lord still waits, He requests our blood

He wants us to work at sacrifice and greed

Learn the difference, ask only for what you need

She spoke of hard times, she spoke to our children

The Lord listens to our cries, as He searches from within

Those who call themselves saved, children of our Lord

Yet how can you be, when sacrifice you can't afford?

The world continues to ask the question why

Only coming to the Lord when they have reason to cry

For those who were blessed with money and power

It is time to own up in the world's darkest hour

When you come to the Lord, it's not what you bring

The question is, are you willing to give up something?

Stranger in the Park

Sitting in the park on this winter day
Watching time slide by, not much to say
A stranger came by and sat next to me
He asked, "Do you know Jesus, the son of Thee?"
I looked at him with a puzzled look
The stranger understood, that was all it took
He asked me have I heard of the Holy Spirit
The stranger then stood up and said, "Son get with it"
He started to get angry, his face grew with fear
As he looked toward the sky, his eyes filled with tears
Lord help this man who sits in the park
Although the sun shines, he sits in the dark
I wonder does he know, I wonder does he feel it
There came a rumble from the clouds, is that the Holy Spirit?
The stranger turned to me, he said "Man, find the Lord
It's something you can't wait for, lost time you can't afford"
He wiped his tears, he then bowed his head
With a sudden chill through his body, his face turned red
The stranger then stated, "Jesus please show him Thee
Give him the vision, allow him to see"
The stranger stood up, raised his hands to the sky
He stated "Jesus died for us and you don't know why!"
He turned to me and said "Son, find the word
Jesus is coming back. Now I know THAT you heard!"

Under Construction

Lord, can you help me? I seem to have lost my way
As the sky opened up, a voice said "Say what you have to say"
I tried to be a person of Christ
My path has been blocked without sacrifice
I allow my greed to get the best of me
Even though I know right from wrong, I still avoid Thee
Each time I try to regroup, I find a path of destruction
My heart cries out, but my soul is under construction
The Holy Spirit came and gave my body its chill
As I thought God left me, the Holy Spirit imposed its will
When you take one step, I take one with you
Believe in Me, that's all I ask you to do
As you go through life, don't allow any obstruction
I know what's in your heart, you're my Christian under construction
So when you seem lost, that's when you call to Me
Look over to your left, and you will see that your spirit walks with Thee
Walk through life with Me, and watch how your life flows
Like my promise to the world, do you see my rainbows?
So don't be shy, just understand your function
For those who seem lost, they are just Christians under construction

Come Visit

Hello people, there's a place downtown
I know you've heard, the coolest place around
People gather from near and far
Some come by train, others use their car
So grab your friends who haven't heard
About this place, so they can hear the Word
Don't be shy, just come and get with it
It's the House that God built, filled with the Holy Spirit
He's given blessings, He's not asking for much
So tell me, people, have you felt His touch?
This place is rocking, people scream and shout
Won't you come on down to see what they're talking about?
The Holy Spirit will change your sight
Don't take any detours, come on down tonight
This isn't a gimmick, this isn't a scam
Come to this place and watch the people jam
Its open tonight, the spirit is live within
So come on people, let your journey begin
Once you feel it, once you allow Him in
Your life will change, are you ready to begin?
The doors are open, I hope you feel it
Trust in Jesus, He is the Holy Spirit

A Stranger Met God

A friendly stranger sat quietly as a mouse

As he took the stage, to address God's house

He spoke of his time when he was sent away

We all listened in shock, on this bright Sunday

His voice was honest as we listened in a daze

He spoke of his experience, as he referred to high praise

God took him to a house where all people seemed to have failed

As he looked to the sky, he said God I don't belong in jail

God placed him there, but never gave a reason

As he entered the big house, it was a whole new season

Scared of his surroundings, he watched all around him in fear

He raised his hands up giving high praise, as his eyes filled with tears

Prisoners approached him to reveal their fears within their hearts

With God's hand on his shoulder, his new role would start

One by one, the stranger listened to their stories

When God told him what to do, he then witnessed God's Glory

Each time he was asked a favor, he felt scared of the task

He would give the Lord high praise, then do as God asked

What started as a few, grew humbled by belief

As God guided the stranger, his heart felt relief

God had taken the stranger from fear to praise

As his members grew in numbers, they followed his ways

Humbled by his new friends, from the house he was sent

The stranger now spreads the word, in memory of where he went

Now Can You See

People often complain of their troubles in time

Yet do they look at how little they do other than whine

Did you wake up this morning? A blessing from me

Go to a graveyard, they didn't, now can you see?

YES LORD!

People often complain of their troubles with food

Yet do they look at the hunger of the world; how rude

Did you go hungry today? You were blessed by me

Go to a starving nation, they did. Now can you see?

YES LORD!

People often complain of what they should cherish

A job, their health, their home, these could all perish

Yet do they say thank you for the blessing from me?

Open your eyes, my children! Now can you see?

YES LORD!

As you walk through life, remember one loss

It wasn't yours; it was my son's blood on the cross

As he gave life, the Holy Spirit embraced thee

Learn of what you could lose, now can you see?

PRAISE GOD!

Goodbye Mom-Hello My Angel

Good morning Lord, I found sadness in my heart

It was a sad day for me from the very start

When I needed love, she gave me her best

On my days of doubt, she would pass any test

FEEL ME LORD

Of all my friends in this God forsaken world

It was mom who was the closest, I called her my girl

No matter what the problem, no matter where I went wrong

She always welcomed me back where I truly belonged

FEEL ME LORD

So Lord I thank you for giving me time to confess

I thank You for the angel who gave my life her best

As she sits beside you, please tell her of my pain

I miss my mom so much, as my face feels her rain

THANK YOU LORD

As the skies opened up, the sunshine came on through

A voice from the skies whispered, "Son, she loved you too

She gave you a path, she gave you her very best

Now she sits beside me, as we lay her soul to rest"

Shake it up

The bishop spoke of an angry Lord
His anger is something this world can't afford
He spoke of change, he felt the need to disrupt
Go against the grain, the Lord wants us to shake it up
He spoke of God's house, this isn't a club
Be careful who you push, be careful who you rub
We shall be checking at the door, checking for fakes
As the Lord shows His anger with powerful earthquakes
Don't come to the Lord's house, if you don't really believe
He sees all the sinners, with something up their sleeves
The bishop spoke in volumes, loudly so you could hear
If you need him to explain, then you should pull up a chair
He spoke of how he traveled with fear in his heart
Yet he believed in Jesus, his savior from the start
"Shake it up" he yelled, don't follow the crowd
The Lord will tell you what He wants, He speaks twice as loud
Give yourself to Him, give Him full praise
He will take you from the night, show you bright sunny days
As I listened to the bishop, I felt tears erupt
I felt God's hand on my shoulder telling me "Shake it up"

A Chosen Angel

Hello people! There's a game today

The Angels are playing on this fine day

But as the Lord counted, He was one angel shy

The Lord looked to the dugout to call on His guy

So without hesitation, He made the call from the sky

Lester was called up to be His new guy

Now, Lester was ready, as he stood real proud

It was Lester's way, as his presence drew a crowd

I am ready, my Lord, as Lester gave Him his stare

The angels were complete, as game time drew near

Lester then smiled, as the angels began to play

Let's remember my friend Lester, on this very sad day

My Testimony

My sick young brother had called out to me

As I entered the hospital, I was escorted by Thee

My brother was saved from his saddened past

He spoke of a church; His soul it had grasped

My brother spoke of the members' open hearts

He said "my brother, go visit, seek a fresh start"

You could see my brother had spoken, while in pain

I promised to visit, as his tears brought the rain

Palm Sunday it was, I showed up with doubt

As I entered His house, people began to shout

They grabbed my hands, formed a circle in praise

A spirit of hope, sent me in a daze

I watched as they prayed for my young sick brother

The Lord was within them, as they prayed to no other

I started to sweat as they prayed for my fears

They continued to pray as my eyes filled with tears

The moment had passed; I sat down to give praise

Filled with emotion, never in my days

Another preacher came and spoke of Thee

She commanded the crowd to change I to We

All who are without the blessing of a job

Raise your hand, whether you're Susan or Bob

Those who are blessed to still be employed

Place your hand on them, as His spirit is deployed

I turned to a lady who stood in the crowd

Placed my hand on her shoulder as she cried aloud

Her body trembled, as she prayed on this day

Scared by her reaction, my heart filled today

Touched by the Lord, I vowed to return

The Lord smiled at me, as I had much to learn

I Know You Can Hear- But Do You Listen?

Today in church, I watched with fear
How many people suffer, how very little care
Many of us call out for the hand of Thee
But when He answers, we act like this can't be
The Lord is forgiving, when we blame His touch
It's not for us to judge, when we ask for so much
Believe in Thee, give Him your praise
Yet when He answers, are we in a daze?
Each Sunday, people visit a church of their choice
But do they really listen, do they hear His voice?
We all have our doubts, we question His direction
Yet we claim to have faith, yet we question His selection
It's not for us to question, or even understand
Even when the Lord gives, we question His plan
Don't look to the sky, don't act like you believe
When the Lord looks inside you, it's Him you can't deceive
So when you visit on Sunday, you claim a pure heart
Listen to the voice who tried to help you from the start
When you had those troubles that your heart couldn't bear
Remember when His voice told you, "I am here"
So, give yourself to Thee, it's Jesus you are missing
I know you can hear Him, but have you been listening?

Don't Say Thanks, Show It

As Thanksgiving Day approaches, do people really care?

Only when they have a problem, they cry "life is unfair"

Only on Sunday do people change their ways

God is a giving God for all seven days

Food is something that we want and need

Yet before every meal, instead of thanks, we show greed

So when tides are requested, we all fall short

As we play judge to others, we cheat the highest court

When we are blessed with family, friends and food

Do we give thanks to God almighty? NO! How rude

God blessed all, but some more than others

Yet we never give thanks to our sisters and brothers

We come every Sunday to God's house to sing praise

Now when it comes to giving, we run out in a blaze

How do we ask a giving God to continue to give?

Yet we all call ourselves Christians, and forget how to live

Let's not forget the person who is not dressed well, but gives all

He meets the sunshine standing ten feet tall

Giving what he has without blinking an eye

Yet those with so much ask the question "why?"

Thanksgiving has a meaning of sharing one's plate

Give to a stranger, it's never too late

The Visit

Last night while I slept, darkness filled the sky

I heard a sound, as I felt my heart cry

Startled and surprised, I woke with a chill

It was then He spoke, "My son remain still"

Like a child, I sat quietly, without a sound

The Lord then spoke, "I am here in your town"

He raised His arms and said "come with me"

Like a child in shock, I walked over to Thee

The room was filled with darkness tonight

But as He spoke, His voice brought on a light

"Be kind to others; walk with your pride high

When others cross you, just look to the sky

It's me, your Lord, who is here by your side

To all I am not seen, they all think I hide

We will walk together, so come take my hand

To all you will seem strange, as they worship my land"

Happy inside, the Lord left without a trace

All I had was the memories and the tears on my face

I had awakened from my dream with my face cherry red

I had feelings of warmth from the visit, while in bed

Trust in Thee

Sunday comes but once a week
On this day, some people turn the other cheek
We come together to give the Lord praise
Sad thing is, we forget the other 6 days
As we gather to listen for the Word
When Monday comes, do you remember what you've heard?
Help me Lord, for the flesh is weak
I need your strength 7 days a week
Suddenly, the clouds cleared the skies
When the sun appeared, water filled my eyes
My legs began to tremble, buckled at the knees
With my arms opened wide, I yelled "Lord please"
His voice came to me, gentle yet stern
You know right from wrong, why don't you learn?
Why do you doubt me outside My home?
Yet on Sunday you call to Me, for your sins to condone?
You sing me praise, you bring your heart
If only my children would listen from the start
I gave you life, I created all
So when it comes to trust, there you fall
I am not a God who works part-time
Learn to trust in me, I will be there every time

Your Hurt Angel

Hello Lord, it's me again

Your true believer, your long lost friend

I come to you with troubles of mind

My soul is confused about these hard times

Your angels have come to spread their wings

Trouble has come, heartaches they bring

I took to you, Lord, with my broken heart

Guide your angel from her troubled start

A rumble came from clear blue skies

My heartbeat increased as temperatures rise

The voice of thee spoke only to me

Listen to your heart as it beats for thee

Your troubles are only those you seek

Look past your eyes, look past this week

Time will pass and darkness will clear

As the Lord spoke my eyes grew a tear

You, my angel, are never alone

I've watched you live, I've see you've grown

Feel the beat of your soul with my heart

They've been as one from the very start.

Your Angel Is Here

Today seemed cloudy as I sat in my car

My mind seemed to wander yet not very far

Soon I would raise my head to the sky

With tears on my face I would ask the Lord why

-Hear Me Lord-

Silence responded yet I couldn't hear a thing

As the clouds brought the rain instead of the spring

Sad for the moment with tears on my face

Again, I would yell what's wrong with this place

-Hear Me Lord-

The lightning rang out as thunder would follow

As the skies remained cloudy the sounds were so hollow

When I looked toward the skies to search for the one

It was then that I realized that His job wasn't done

-Hear Me Lord-

So I started to walk down some lonely street

It was then I was joined by a 2nd pair of feet

Scared by the steps with no one in sight

There came a voice that said it's alright

-Hear Me Lord-

No matter your worries there is always someone worse

But when you needed one, it was you who would curse

Before you give up or do something you'll regret

Your angel watches over you with every single step

The Challenge

A challenge was issued from the pastor today
As we sat and listened, on this blessed Sunday
He spoke of living like the Holy One
Living without sin, yet still having fun
While blasting those who sing and falsely give praise
The challenge was put down for all 7 days
His words rang out; it's going to be tough
Roll up your sleeves, you haven't done enough
As he spoke of the Lord, his voice went loud
Preaching the word, with support from the clouds
He issued a challenge to those in God's house
It doesn't matter if you wear a shirt or a blouse
Did you give yourself to Jesus, did you commit?
Don't wait for tomorrow, it's time to submit
He spoke of others, how they spoke of high praise
Are you a true believer, or just going through a phase?
As you come to the Lord's house to sing and give tides
Are you a true believer, what does your heart truly hide?
As he stood before all and talked of a fight
Prepare for the battle, it will take day and night
The devil is busy taking all the sinners in the land
As the Lord stands before us, will you take His hand?

Did You Forget?

I woke up this morning, a blessing indeed

Taking for granted, showing my greed

Rising from bed, starting my day

Forgetting the most important thing, forgetting to pray

I started my day by getting something to eat

Forgetting to be grateful that I could rise to my feet

I proceeded to get dressed, planning my day

Again forgetting the most important thing, forgetting to pray

My day was fruitful with plenty of fun

Again forgetting the most important thing, giving praise to the one

Came home from work and was greeted with love

Again forgetting the most important thing, the one from above

As you can see, a person can remember his day

So tell me why we can't remember to pray?

The Lord only asks that we allow Him into our hearts

As you can see, we rarely do our part

Yet when we have a problem, when we are faced with grief

This is when we remember His name, only for relief

Open your hearts; allow Him your full praise

You seek Him full-time to forgive you for your sinful ways

Your Angel

The Lord has listened to you cry

The nights you wished and wondered why

Each time you reached, you did with fear

The Lord has shown you He's always there

He sent me here to ease your pain

To walk with you to feel the rain

Since every drop that hits your face

He sent me a girl to take His place

As life goes on, you should believe

His love's no trick, check my sleeve

I've heard your cries through the nights

I know your fears and your frights

Your angel girl wants you to know

Be yourself, don't be a show

As you believe you'll show the world

You have an angel; a precious pearl.

<u>Why</u>

Crowds had gathered for a very sad occasion

A couple so happy had met a new invasion

As people came together, the preacher yelled why

As sadness had fallen upon, all the people began to cry

WHY?

My Lord, please take them in your hands

Bless their love, make me understand

We all have our time, no matter how short

To do your deeds, this too we must sort

WHY?

Asked the preacher, did her time come so fast?

Is there something we should know, or should we not ask?

This couple that you take to bless in your grace

As tears began to run down her pretty face

WHY?

Is the question that all want to know

To be blessed with your love is the way to go

You see, why is a question that never seems to end

Can you please tell me why you've taken my good friend?

WHY?

Do we assume that sadness means goodbye?

This couple that we speak of got married – asked me why

It was sad because their freedom had come to an end

They loved each other so deeply the Lord yelled

AMEN

The Lord's in Touch

As the sky cleared - the Lord called to me

He said, be patient for all of man to see

As I laid in bed with a tear on my face

The Lord called to me; come over my place

He said that my soul seemed to need His hand

I agreed with my Lord as I quickly rose like a man

Yes, I said to God, guide me to Your sky

I've been lost without you, Lord, as I began to cry

He placed his arm around me as we walked down this road

He told me to rejoice, He would release me of my load

Trouble has been around for as long as Adam and Eve

So understand what I want as He made me believe

Life is too short, I would like you to have some fun

Slow down from this world, remember number one

I have my son so that people would understand my hurt

But instead of love and belief, they've turned my name to dirt

They lie to me, they curse me without a single thought

But when they have some trouble, it's their soul I've brought

Please Lord, they cry, help me in my time of need

Only want me when you need me? Now who has the greed?

But I am the Lord, I forgive all who ask

Despite how they deceive me, now this must be a task.

The Devil In Town

On this cold night, she wore a frown

And on this day, it's Devil's town

He came today to raise the stakes

To show us all just what it takes

He offers you all fool's gold

A false promise will be told

He comes today to grant you a wish

You must comply and serve his dish

The Devil makes no type of plea

After your one wish you belong to thee

Forget your God, forget your faith

Come to me with what you're worth

I offer you so much, my friend

The rules for you, I'll make them bend

Temptation, flirtation, or even gold

Could not replace what may unfold

Since I've granted you one wish

You are now food upon my dish

Since you gave me food for thought

The Devil's in town for what he's brought

Understand his rules, they are for keeps

Your soul, your belief, your heart, he reaps.

The Devil's Call

Now listen, for it's you I've come to take

Although you pray to God, it's your soul that's at stake

So before you go off crying of the love you've lost

You should have thought this through, now look at what it cost

Just because you love someone, doesn't make it right

Remember what you have, before you lose it tonight

Those feelings that you have, that selfish little pride

Won't be worth a thing when you've lost your hide

You need to listen to your love, when he does complain

I know he is unruly, I know he is a pain

But if you love him, then listen to his request

Because once he's gone, you'll miss his very best

Now don't you worry, the Devil's on the phone

The Lord gave you inner beauty, but I'll make you be alone

So go ahead my dear, just stick to what you like

The Devil's got you another man after this one takes a hike

Men are all over a dime a dozen, for your needs

Now don't expect feelings, it's you who has this greed\

I can't promise you love, you should have kept your ex

So now that you've released him to go to another

You still have your selfish ways while he'll want no other

Yes he still loves you, but I've sent him away

Although it's my call, you wanted life this way.

Last Night

Last night I heard a quiet gentle cry
It was your heart, and I could only wonder why
Last night you lay sleepless in your bed
The Lord called to me; your love had not been fed
Last night an angel came to me to learn
The Lord had called on her, He too had concern
While you were there asleep, quiet without a trace
The angels circled high, to see the tears on your face
A smile you may wear, does not show what's inside
The angel that had come, looked at your foolish pride
Last night you called out loudly; "Why must I cry?"
The angel, sad for a moment, said "I cannot tell a lie"
You, my pretty one, have a man who loves you true
Now, he too has a past that neither of you can get through
Both of you must face, what is past must remain
If you don't leave it there, you will only bring pain
I have brought you both together and offer no better choice
So try to look at your heart and listen to My voice
Last night you both cried in different beds, you see
It was strange, yet rewarding; you both cried to Me
A woman has her feelings, she feels them deep inside
And when she hunts for love, this too she cannot hide
A man has his feelings, but he allows manhood to prevail
Like a boat without its wind, it will never set sail
You both need each other, so stop these foolish games
Last night you were both hurt, no matter who's to blame
I only offer this, as an angel, I know love
And you both have good roots, the Lord grew you from above

Is One Day Too Much to Give?

Funny how Sunday makes people think of our Lord

Some have good thoughts, that we too must applaud

Church is our temple, we've all come to give grace

Some come to learn of His love on their face

God is our Lord, although our religions aren't the same

We keep our own faith as the Lord listens without shame

On Sunday, we give thanks, we all bow our heads

Whather to give thanks for the living, or memories of our dead

Now what we must learn is that life has its own worth

It may be precious and short lived on this place we call Earth

Make the best of your time because all else that you do

We'll(?) be a memory or a blessing from the ones you hold true

So if not but for a minute, take time to say a prayer

To the one who gave you life, even when you didn't care

Did you know, every time you needed him, he was always there?

Whether you were grateful or you refused to even share?

Six days you did your best in your own little way

He gave you space and He never said you must pray

So if you're the one who only comes on Sunday by persuasion

Or are you one who may visit only for a special occasion

The Lord watches, He loves, and yes, He still remains

He gave His son for you, can you really feel his pain?

A Talk With Thee

Good morning Lord, can I have a moment of your time?

As the clouds moved apart, a voice stated "fine"

Lord, we as your children, walk this Earth in fear

With His hand on my shoulder, my eyes filled with tears

You, my son, are wrong. My children are never alone

I am here when you call, I hear when you moan

Came and walk with Thee, I have a message for your heart

Pull up a chair, my son, now where should I start?

Each person in this world is given a noble choice

It is ME in their soul when they hear that little voice

As time passes by, people should look toward the sky

Whether they are looking for love, or just asking the question "why?"

Tomorrow is not promised, so enjoy each and every day like it is your last

Live for the moment, and try to forget the troubles of your past

My son, I hear all of those who pray each and every day

My plan for all of my children, will be shown to all in God's way

So, like lost sheep, you may wander throughout these troubled lands

But remember one thing. You left your trust in God's hands

As I turned away, the clouds cleared the skies

The sun shined on through, as my heart began to cry

Thank you, my Lord, for the time that we had

You've uplifted my spirit, and for this I am glad

A Look at Life from Thee

Last night while winter's cold came to visit

There was a silent moment, and my mind asked "who is it?"

While all seemed quiet, without any light

The Lord came by to visit me last night

Dreams are windows that we all should not ignore

Like moments in life that come through any door

Treat every moment like you want it to last

Every troubled moment may seem like a task

Come walk with me through the windows of life

With the Lord's embrace, I made no sacrifice

We walked together, His spirit and my soul

As He graced my presence, our story would unfold

We seemed to walk through the sad moments of my past

As time went on, the Lord stated they wouldn't last

As the windows of life allow us to look through

Like a child on Christmas, I was excited by the view

I looked at the story with tears on my face

With the Lord's presence, my past increased its pace

I turned to the Lord to ask Him a question

But before I could speak, a voice drew my attention

The Lord was gone from my side, without a trace

It was His voice from the wind that left tears on my face

The voice of Thee stated I am here when you need

Remember your past and don't get caught up in the greed

Speak to Me, Lord

Hello, my Lord, I seem lost in this world

Yet only with you do I feel like a girl

Although I walk with my head held high

Deep in my heart, my soul wants to cry

HEAR ME, LORD!

All through my life I came to you for support

Yet sometimes in life you protected me life a fort

Placed your walls around me to keep me from harm

You always warned me as you set off my alarms

HEAR ME, LORD!

My family has been here all through my life

I'll always remember my place as a wife

My children are fine, I thank you, my Lord

For my health and my children I too must applaud

HEAR ME, LORD!

The Lord came to me with his arms open wide

He spoke, come my dear, your pain can't hide

You've been good through your life, so please calm your fears

The Lord then spoke, as my eyes grew tears

WITH HIS ARMS AROUND ME!

We walked down His road, He asked me to speak

As my eyes shed a tear, they ran down on my cheeks

I said to my Lord, why is there so much pain?

As He opened His arms, the clouds let it rain

He spoke, you must feel pain before the sun shines on you

As the clouds cleared the skies, the Lord blessed me too.

Top Sheep Dog

Today was a day that **TOP SHEEP DOG** gave his word
He addressed the congregation so he could be heard
The topic was deep yet oh so direct
As he started out soft, his words had their effect
He stated his claim, make no mistake
TOP SHEEP DOG was angry, as his house needed to awake
He made his word loud, but oh so clear
Not in God's house, would he allow you to fear
Talk and gossip have let people's trust sway
TOP SHEEP DOG was angry on God's blessed Sunday
People have the decision of choice
So make the right one, do you hear my voice?
Elders talk to these children of tomorrow
Half dressed girls, boys dressed for jail and their look of sorrow
The Lord gave us 7 days to a week
Live like the Lord, don't wait until Sunday to turn your cheek
As **TOP SHEEP DOG** spoke of his plans
He announced this is God's house, and respect the demands
So go, God's children, think of my words
Remember this day, remember what you've heard
TOP SHEEP DOG is watching at the top of the hill
This is my watch, as you could feel God's will

Choices

A child is born with hope and with fear
Parents are blessed, as they both shed a tear
As children grow older, as they listen and learn
Sometimes things are great, sometimes they turn
A child doesn't choose his parents, you see
They grow up with love or hatred, and flee
Trapped inside of a victim of hate
Before they can grow, they are doomed by their fate
Some learn of hope, when they listen to a voice
Others land in jail, with very little choice
A child inside, seeks help from his grief
As the Lord reaches out to offer relief
There's always hope if we listen to His voice
No matter the situation, we always have a choice
Lost children of the world seek the love of our Lord
Not the father they were given, but one they can applaud
Lost children are those who wander in the dark
As they go place to place, in the devil's park
The Lord calls to them to show His light
Yet they ignore his call, and continue to fight
So follow the Lord, listen to His voice
Remember my children, we all have a choice.

I Have a Question

I have a question, I seem so confused
Do I go to church, do I pay my dues?
Lord I have a question, I want to follow Thee
Do I go to church, is my soul always free?
Lord I have a question, I need to find your path
Do I go to church to avoid the Devil's wrath?
As I looked to the sky, I questioned no more
When the clouds released a rumble, I headed for the door
You, my son, have asked questions of Thee
So listen for the answers, are you afraid of Me?
I've always called, but you never seemed to hear
So now you answer, that's what brings my fear
All your life, you didn't walk with Thee
You spoke of belief, but acted against Me
Since you've changed your life, and gave yourself to Thee
I have taken all your troubles, they are here with Me
You may not get your needs when you ask
But I am Lord Almighty, I take on any task
All your questions are answered with trust of Thee
So the real question is; do you trust Me?

I Prayed Last Night

I come to worship you Lord, I sing and give you praise
As I come before You, I bow down all 7 days
Your word is your bond, as I turns to we
So I proudly surrender my soul to worship Thee
Lord you are full of mercy, so I worship you
Please lead my path, so I can learn what to do
We are lambs, as we wander through Your lands
Only to return with praise of Your guiding hands
As I sat up, Lord, and stared into the night
It was then I realized I live by faith, not sight
I believe You are holy, I believe in Thee
One day I will understand why you saved a wretch like me
That's when a chill went through me from within
Followed by a tear, as my face wore a grin
A voice in my head spoke ever so loud
You gave yourself to Me, and for this I am so proud
Go into the land, I've blessed you with My word
Give praise to the Lord, find those who haven't heard
Let them read the Word, let them learn of Me
I am the Holy Spirit, tell them you've heard from Thee

My Brother Vincent

Hello-have you met my younger brother?
His name is Vincent, caring like no other
When someone called him for help, he came
Never to be judged, never to be blamed
He's been through a lot, some call it thick and thin
Until you know his life, don't judge him
Today you see him fighting a battle of life
He has my support and a loving wife
Today you see him fighting the devil every day
It was God who told all, there is no way
Vincent lived a troubled life in his past
The Lord stepped in, He said your troubles won't last
The Vincent I know is strong with a big heart
Fighting for his life, scared from the start
The doctors told him, you don't have a chance
That's when God stepped in, I'll take this dance
When they only gave him 3 weeks to live
It was God's voice which said I will always forgive
From a troubled childhood to one tough life in the streets
To kindness to offer to whomever he meets
So when you meet Vincent, please shake his hand
Then you will see his smile, so you will understand
A man who had the devil, but God gave him vision
Now he has hope, he made the right decision

Have Faith

The Lord paid a visit through my Spirit today
We walked through the halls knowing His way
My brother lay sick in his hospital bed
Saddened by his health with his eyes colored red
As I appeared, it brought a smile to his face
Hello Vincent, don't give up on this place
He spoke of the Devil who visited him today
Informed him you're not sick, listen to what I say
I know of what I speak, don't listen to any other
Not your Bishop, your friends, the Doctor or your brother
Take some vitamins, some juices, and water
Pack up your bags, leave this house of slaughter
My brother began to believe what the Devil had said
Forgetting he was a Christian, as he lay in his bed
I yelled at him, how could you lose faith in the Lord?
Don't you remember? To lose faith you cannot afford
The Devil's a liar, but you must truly believe
It's his deceit that he wears on his sleeve
The next day the Bishop came and spoke the same words
Two messengers of the Lord, I hope that he heard
We can only hope that his Spirit is awakened
By the word from our Lord, which he has forsaken
To lose faith is a path that no one can defend
If you believe in the Holy Spirit, then you have a true friend

Blessed By Tina

Today in my visit I met a young lady named Tina
With a very soft voice, tell me, have you seen her?
She spoke of my brother, how he came into her heart
I asked her to tell me her story from the very start
She said it started while she was new
Unable to help Vincent, until she learned what to do
New at her location, but skilled by her profession
She became close with my brother, but never revealed her confession
One day as she passed by Vincent's room he called out
When she responded, what are you yelling about?
She said he told her to come now and please listen
He said I have something to share, you know I'm a Christian
The sadness you are going through, all your troubles will pass
The Lord revealed, don't worry, your sadness won't last
She listened to Vincent, as her eyes drew her tears
Relieved of her sadness, the Spirit removed her fears
Soon she was called on to perform a task on my brother
As others were called upon, my brother would allow no other
Tina looked at the papers and noticed something was wrong
The stats showed danger, even when others felt so strong
She revealed the mistake that could have killed my brother
The Doctors, the head nurses all gave praise like no other
Tina was honored for saving a life on that day
With tears in her eyes, her heart wanted to pray
The next morning, Tina passed by Vincent's room with a smile
As Vincent saw her, he yelled out like a child
"Tina, did you know that they almost killed me last night?
But some nurse found the problem, and made things alright."
With tears in her eyes, she smiled at him
Never telling her story, she just stared with a grin

Forgive

Did you ever wonder why we always relive our hurt?
It's because we don't forgive, we just keep dishing the dirt
The pain that we encounter is pain of the heart
Did you really forgive? Do you want a new start?
It's like a cut that you place a band aid on to heal
Yet if you don't leave it alone, it's the pain you will still feel
Until we learn to forgive and learn to forget
The pain we shall keep, it's the pain we shall regret
Close your eyes to what has happened to you
Now this won't be easy, but this you must do
Because until you learn to change how you live
The hurt and anger won't allow you to forgive
Now don't ask that person to apologize to you
Just be the strong one, this will be so hard to do
As you start to forgive without seeking anything in return
Your soul will heal from the hurt and the pain
So learn to smile, it's for you to turn the other cheek
As you learn to forgive, it's your happiness you seek
So take my hand and let's learn how to live
As we enjoy our new journey, as we learn to forgive

Mistakes

We all seem to think we've gotten everything right
Yet when we get the results, we are wrong like day to night
We all seem to think we walk tall and strong
Yet when we get the results, some rights are so wrong
When all we need to do is sit and listen
It's the word of the Spirit that we have been missing
As we go through life, we raise the stakes
Yet humbled by His word, admitting our mistakes
The Lord only requires that you live as Thee
Forgive those who hurt you Lord, how can this be?
A voice then came and spoke of the stakes
I forgave you for your sins, I forgave your mistakes
So if I, the Lord, can give you a chance
Why do you feel you can't go another dance?
Lift up your heart, forgive those with a grudge
Only I am the Lord, who are you to judge?
So, the next time you feel better than another
Remember My word, and just forgive your brother
For when you do this, your Spirit can raise the stakes
As you walk with Thee, doesn't He forgive your mistakes?

A Miracle From Myrtle Beach

Can I Tell you about Lilly, who chose no fear?
As I watched her rise from her wheelchair
Clemon, her husband, who seemed strong from within
Yet I felt he also had a story of where he had been
Now Lilly was a pretty lady, who told of her past
With the Lord in her corner, she knew her troubles wouldn't last
Lilly called herself a miracle, as her smile lit the sky
Happy for her blessings, and not ashamed to tell you why
She spoke of how her doctors told her that children for her couldn't be
But Lilly believed in the Lord, and the Lord said "Walk with me"
As Lilly grew stronger, with the Lord by her side
Whenever she had doubt, the Lord reached down to help her stride
Lilly talked of a feeling she felt from a stranger named Clemon
What the Lord revealed to her, they would be like tea with lemons
He was a man who needed to be shown he was chosen
So every other path he'd choose, the Lord made sure it was frozen
He spoke of a deal that he felt the Lord couldn't do
As the Lord revealed His hand, it was clear that He'd picked you
So today we met Lilly, blessed with a man who loves to preach
As we sat at their table with the miracles of Myrtle Beach

Tears of Glory

Close your eyes and remember the face of a child
Innocent in every way, this should cause a smile
As a child looks at you, it's for guidance and direction
With love in your heart, your child seeks your affection
Being a man or a woman, we are humbled by Thee
So who am I to question what the Lord asks of me?
The Lord never told us that we should live in fear
Yet when I raise my head to Him, my eyes shed a tear
I was once ashamed when I felt a tear in my eye
But it was by God's hand that raised the question, why?
When you shed a tear at the thought of Thee
It's your spirit He's captured, your troubles are free
So each time you cry, remember your sad days
While the Lord has your back, so give Him your praise
Do you feel your world changing, do you feel His glory?
What was once your sadness; you should now have a new story
So raise your hands high, as you look to the sky
As you sing the Lord praise, your heart will know why

Together We Could Be Stronger

Time is short for all on Earth
Yet we take for granted what life is worth
Each day we awaken is a day we should rejoice
Because one day the Lord may take away that choice
We just expect life to continue, with hope for more
Until the unforeseen opens up a darkened door
Some go to church to look for a new day
Others believe in their hearts, but refuse to pray
We never know the path that we will take
Until life shows us our next mistake
If we could just stop, and walk the footsteps of another
Then we might see a different life, and call all our brother
You never understand today, until you live through tomorrow
Life will bring happiness, also it will bring you sorrow
If we all could take a moment to give thanks to Thee
Then together we could learn, and "I" could turn to "we"
So let's walk together to face the path of fear
Since without faith of Thee, none of us would be here

Your Angel Is Here

Today seemed cloudy as I sat in my car

My mind seemed to wander yet not very far

Soon I would raise my head to the sky

With tears on my face I would ask the Lord why

-Hear Me Lord-

Silence responded yet I couldn't hear a thing

As the clouds brought the rain instead of the spring

Sad for the moment with tears on my face

Again, I would yell what's wrong with this place

-Hear Me Lord-

The lightning rang out as thunder would follow

As the skies remained cloudy the sounds were so hollow

When I looked toward the skies to search for the one

It was then that I realized that His job wasn't done

-Hear Me Lord-

So I started to walk down some lonely street

It was then I was joined by a 2nd pair of feet

Scared by the steps with no one in sight

There came a voice that said it's alright

-Hear Me Lord-

No matter your worries there is always someone worse

But when you needed one, it was you who would curse

Before you give up or do something you'll regret

Your angel watches over you with every single step

He Chose Me

All throughout my life, I knew of Thee
Yet little did I know, that He chose me
As we live our life, we seek knowledge from within
Yet little do we know, it's His work we shall begin
Now some people count their fortune as lucky
Yet little did I realize, it's because He chose me
As we go through life wishing for better days
We forget to give thanks, we forget to give praise
Do you ever sit and think of all that could be?
Yet with all the sorrow in the world, He chose me
Even though we have more than we really need
It's our forgetting to be grateful, it's all about greed
Yet even after we forget of God's giving grace
We judge all others without knowing our place
I feel there is a purpose, that one day will be clear
It's His voice that guides me; it's His voice I hear
No longer a stranger, I now listen to Thee
I've been blessed by my Lord, I'm glad He chose me

I Decided To Pray

Today I met a man who had a story to tell
So I pulled up a chair, so I could listen very well
He took a second to gather himself
As he began to speak, you could see his wealth
He spoke of a boy who jumped to 6 foot 7
As he told his story, he spoke of the blessing from heaven
When he was a boy, he played basketball
Skilled beyond his years, as he could recall
He always played with the older kids
While strangers didn't know, his friends placed their bids
He continued to play as he went to school
Not forgetting the Lord, his golden rule
One day he was supposed to play his biggest game
Instead of him practicing, he sat down with no shame
He sat on the bench worried about his funds
Knowing he had the skills, knowing his shot had the guns
While the other teammates practiced for the big game
Roger just sat, as he prayed with no shame
Scouts from all over came to see them play
What they didn't understand, was why he acted this way
Roger went on to play his best game with pride
He had the Holy Spirit, a blessing he couldn't hide
His teammates and friends asked what happened that day
Roger answered, instead of practice, I decided to pray

The Faith of Roger's Mother

Now people you should listen to this story I heard

It was one of a man's past, as he spoke of the word

As he sat in his chair, you could see in his face

Roger was about to take me to his hidden place

When he started to talk, he adjusted his chair

As he started to speak, his eyes drew tears

He spoke of when he was a little lad

It was just him and his mom, that's all he had

He spoke of how his mother always prayed to the Lord

Yet he never did without, even if they couldn't afford

His mother always gave her tides without holding out.

Her heart was pure, the Lord had no doubt

One day, his mother came home with tears in her eyes

She said, son, we have no choice, I can't tell you any lies

We need help, our money isn't enough to live

I prayed to my Lord, as she still had to give

His mother was a proud lady, she never wanted to apply

Yet the day had come, when she could no longer deny

The mailman had delivered a check to his home

He opened the mail, then called his mom on the phone

Mother, please come home from work, hurry, don't delay

She said the bus doesn't come now, say what you must say

Roger yelled, mom, don't take a bus, take a taxi!

She said, son, what is wrong that you truly need me?

Mom, we received a check, it's addressed to you and me

We are no longer poor, as his mother said, how could this be?

A family in need received the Lord's blessing that day

As his mother's tears on her face allowed her to pray

53

Bound By Grace

Today was a day a real lesson came to me

It was about learning the true meaning of the phrase "Lord have mercy"

There was a story that brought tears to my face

I learned about mercy, and about God's saving grace

It was a story about a white man who was filled with rage

His life was a living hell, as he remained in his own cage

He was forced to work with a black man, who believed in the Holy Spirit

The white man asked for a transfer, but the boss wouldn't hear it

This white man always spoke of his household in disarray

While the black man kept telling him, "friend, you need to pray"

The black man continued to preach to him, but to no avail

As his new friend's rage just kept him inside his own jail

Until one day, this angry man was humbled a bit

This was due to his only son getting very sick

It was then he ran to church, this to him was a strange place

His newfound friend joined him with tears on his face

This white man turned to his black friend and asked "please pray with me"

Together they kneeled before God, and begged for mercy

He gave himself to Jesus, as he prayed for his only son

His newfound friend told him, "now your new journey has begun"

The black man asked the doctor "check me for the blood you need"

As the doctor's eyes opened wide, his son would no longer bleed

Now two total strangers became great friends, in a new place

As this angry gentleman learned about God's giving grace

Save Me Lord

Take my hand Lord, and please show me your way
Because I seemed to be lost, it seems like yesterday
As I have gone through life, I haven't listened to your word
It's why I seem lost, acting like I haven't heard
We are your children, we cannot exist without you
So when we stray from your word, show us what to do
Now, I know you continue to bless all, even those who stray
So tonight I kneel before you, learning how to pray
Like any children, we are always in need of your blessed hand
No matter how grown we might be, we still don't know your plan
Even those who sin and seek the Holy Ghost
Lord, help them even more, because they need you the most
As we ask your forgiveness, we can only hope you hear
Seeking the hand of you, my Father, as we all shed a tear
So tonight I kneel before you, as I cry to Thee
Take my hand o'Lord, and save a wretch like me

What You Gonna Do?

Now Easter Sunday is for you and me
But the real meaning is for the Resurrection of Thee
Some go to church, yet they haven't a clue
Remember my question: What you gonna do?
You can enter a church and learn about Thee
Or you can simply go to set your mind free
Some feel that if they spend a Sunday or two
You must still face my question "What you gonna do?"
You are required to believe and give with your heart
There is only one heaven, but it requires a new start
When you go to church you might find heartache and bliss
But if you trust in the Lord, He will tell you "I got this"
So look to the sky with a tear on your face
Because you will feel His touch, as you surrender your space
You will meet some who can only speak of what they've heard
Acknowledge the Lord, spread His meaning, and spread His word
As He reaches down to give His helping hand to you
You will be faced with my question "What you gonna do?"

Jehovah

Psalm 83:18

Good afternoon everyone who has opened their eyes

This was a blessing, but was it really a surprise?

The Lord asked a question of both you and me

A question so simple, yet we answer certainly

The question He asks should make everyone think

Yet it has so much power, it could have your mind shrink

How well do you know God, the one titled our Lord?

Or are you just a person who stands to applaud?

Do you realize that "God almighty" is a title created by man?

How well do you know our Lord? Do you really understand?

When you meet a stranger, don't you ask for their name?

So, why when you refer to God, won't you do the same?

The Spirit of God lives full time within him or her

God knows your name, and His is Jehovah

The Devil's World

(John 12-31)

News flash everyone who doesn't understand this world

Crime, murder, rape are offered to all boys and girls

This world that we live in is a world filled with crime

How did this all happen in our life and time?

We were all told that Jehovah rules the Earth

Yet if you read the bible, you will understand it started from birth

I am sure you've heard the story of how the serpent tricked Eve

Since she believed in Satan, it was God's punishment she would receive

Jehovah allowed Satan to tempt man to live his way

So He could teach a lesson, God allowed Earth to be Satan's prey

Jehovah doesn't allow bad things to happen without a reason

While man suffers for his sins, The Lord prepares for a new season

Trust in God and He will protect His children at any cost

While some pray for His forgiveness, others still seem so lost

The world is on a course of self-destruction, as we were told

While Jehovah watches His children escape the devil's hold

So trust His word, my friends and family, as the end is near

It is God's voice of promise that you will soon hear

Devil Means Slanderer

(Genesis 3:1-5)

Good morning my friends who seek knowledge and reason

We all have hope for a blessing in our new season

Yet there is always trouble of which we cannot foresee

That is when we call out to our Father known as Thee

We are told of the devil, and he is called the evil one

While we try to live right, the devil means slanderer

This is his action which could come from him or her

When you have someone who slanders another with hate

They have brought the devil to show their own fate

Did you know that Satan means "the opposer"?

This is what he is to God, the one we know as Jehovah

So when you find someone who tries to change your path

Please pay attention, please beware their wrath

The devil uses anyone who he can, to get his way

Have you become his victim of deceit for today?

Remember the devil was once an angel in heaven

Pay attention to the signs because you don't know what you are getting

I warn you there is a devil who waits for you and me

So always trust your Father as He shows His mercy

The devil will wait. He has plans for your soul

So remember my warning, and let your Father set your goals

Why Are You Afraid?

Good afternoon everybody within the sound of my voice

Are you really afraid? Do you really have a choice?

Each time we wake up to start a new day

Do you stop to say thank you? Do you even pray?

I want you to think about what you hear on the news

Do you stop to think about your life? Do you listen to the clues?

I want you to pay attention to what happens every day

Scary how things happen without a reason, I must say

How often does trouble find you? How does it find your path?

Scary how you feel picked on, but do you do the math?

How often does it seem like life has taken a bad turn?

What has to happen to you, before you finally learn?

Like anything in life, it's your dues that must get paid

Why are you so stubborn? Or are you really afraid?

Do you ever think about where you are heading in life?

Are you afraid of the answer, or the sacrifice?

Do you ever think about where you would be?

If the Lord didn't step in to help a wretch like you or me

Do you ever think about the path Jehovah laid?

Think about my question! Why are you afraid?

The Set-Up

Now people, I have a message to pass on

It is not about how life is, it is not about who belongs

Did you ever wonder why things happen to you?

You feel you're living right. What else must you do?

Did you ever ask the question "Why do things happen to me?

Why do others get the breaks? What is it I cannot see?"

Did you ever sit alone to calm down before you erupt?

You are part of God's plan; you are part of His big set-up

Our Lord allows things to happen for His own reason

Like anything in life, we must prepare for a new season

Our Lord allows things to happen, so that we can call His name

Whether it is for help, or to simply give Him the blame

What you must realize, is that we have a God who loves to hear praise

Since He knows how you will respond, He brings trouble to your days

Because when He lifts you out of your troubled path

That is usually when we seek His hand to rescue us from the devil's wrath

So when you realize God only gives you trouble you can handle

Whether it is hard times, or gossip, or a scandal

You will know His plan is to put you in a time of need or disarray

Because it is part of the Lord's set-up, for you to kneel and pray

Jealousy Brings Envy

Good morning everyone, this message today should make you think

It was a powerful message that could put life on the brink

The bishop engaged everyone to question how their life could be

He challenged us to question if we have jealousy or envy

Now when you have jealousy, it is because you want something so bad

Jealousy is so powerful because it can make a happy man sad

Those people who envy you are angry because you are blessed

Don't ask them why they hate, because this is something they won't confess

Have you ever noticed when you gain something, how people's attitudes change?

They have become jealous of your opportunity, and want their own exchange

Have you ever noticed that as long as you were sad or seemed depressed

Those people were happy for you, and only wished you the best?

Yet if they saw an opportunity for you to rise and smile

They would put you down and judge you, like a child

What you must realize, is the Lord gives you a path with doors

While some open with blessings, haters want what is yours

So I warn you, don't allow jealousy to take away your smile

Accept your blessings that God has presented to you, just like a newborn child

A real friend won't judge what you do or enjoy

They will wish you blessings with your new found joy

So tonight when you lay down, thank God for what has come to be

Don't fall victim to those who are jealous and filled with envy

Help Me

Good morning everyone who has a problem they cannot solve

To those folks who need a miracle, or hope their problems will dissolve

How often do you call on the Lord to rescue you?

Yet you fail to give Him praise, a simple thing you won't do

Now you have met a new problem, and you wonder how this could be

As you bow your head with tears, asking the Lord to "please help me"

Now I know we all fall short when it comes to giving praise

Yet you still only come to His house, when you are having troubled days

Or are you one who always cries out when you have a need?

Yet when you are given help, that is when your response is "yes indeed"

Praise is the answer to get the Lord's direct attention

Not only when things are right; or did I forget to mention?

Praise Him when you can't begin to understand why

Not seeing your blessing when you want it, isn't a reason to cry

All of your life, the Lord has been there by your side

Without you even asking, or when you've kept living with your foolish pride

So, since you will not praise Him, you'll ask "how could this be?"

Problems begin to happen until you cry out "Lord Help Me!"

GOD is GOOD

Hello everyone who has ever questioned our Lord

This is a dangerous thing to do, a move you cannot afford

I am sure you've heard the expression "God is Good" many a time

Yet there are some who don't believe, and that is their crime

I want you to look at the word "good", to see how it is spelled

You can't say "good" without saying "God" the bishop yelled

Take away one "O" from the word known as "good"

Some are superstitious, and would rather knock on wood

Yet when you remove an "O" from "Good", you will find God

How many would rather use a cell phone, or maybe their iPod?

Yet people don't have a problem mentioning how good God is

As long as they receive a blessing or when He takes care of their biz

But God is always there, even when you have your doubt

Not only when things are good, but while you scream and shout

Trust in Him. That is all He has ever asked of you

Yet you still have doubt, when you don't know what to do

It is sad when you cry, because you feel that you try so hard

Remember to praise Him for your life; the gift you disregard

The Cage

Good morning everyone who is within the sound of my voice

You have made your decision, but did you make the right choice?

This message we heard was so powerful that it brought tears

It was one which spoke volumes; it brought a reminder of my years

Today's message might cause you to go into a rage

It was a reminder of how we all live in life's cage

We are all programmed from early childhood of dos and don'ts

Each time we've tried to change, our thoughts have said it won't

How long will you live with the restrictions of the cage?

When will you trust our Lord and turn to the next page?

How long will you be afraid to reach for a better tomorrow?

Will you continue to be a caged animal drowning in your sorrow?

Many people blame their childhood on why they live with restrictions

Yet you are now an adult with your own contradictions

How long will you remain locked up in your own cage?

Living a life of sadness, refusing to turn to the next page

Like any animal that is locked up from birth

Never able to wander free to find his true worth

Step out from the bondage that was set in your mind

Reach for the heavens, your true blessing won't be hard to find

Or you can remain sad and never turn from life's sad page

Blaming the world for your captivity in the cage!

Follow Your Instinct

Good morning my friends who have a lion in you

Do you feel him roar, yet you don't know what to do?

The message today was one that I will remember

It spoke about our instincts that follow every member

Do you ever get a feeling that there is more to life?

Are you a strong woman, or just some man's wife?

Do you feel you have more inside to give?

Are you putting life on hold because someone tells you how to live?

Do you feel like you have so much built up inside?

Yet you allow others to tell you how to live and hide?

Why do you allow the people around you to dictate how you live?

While they enjoy everyday life, it's your spirit that won't forgive

Why do you stay trapped inside of your own mind?

While others see your strength, it's your soul you cannot find

Why do you suppress your thoughts and how you think?

Learn to listen to your feelings by following your own instinct

Until you learn how to walk with confidence in yourself

How can you expect others to acknowledge your true wealth?

Clear Your Clutter

Now today's message was so deep from the start

It was a word that was spoken out from the Lord's heart

The bishop yelled out, and trust me, he didn't stutter

As he cleared his throat, he yelled "clear your clutter"

Now many of you here are still living in your past

Why are you still angry with the one you couldn't grasp?

Are you still upset about how you were treated?

Stop yelling with anger; it's time for you to be seated

Are you still trying to impress someone from your past?

They don't care about you anymore, what part don't you grasp?

Are you still upset about someone who is now dead?

When will you move on and put your emotions to bed?

The clutter in your life consists of the sad moments you've hung onto

Now it's time to move on from your clutter of what life has brought you through

With each moment in life, comes a lesson you should learn

Don't hang onto disappointment; life is a lesson at every turn

Until you learn how to speak out without a hesitation or a stutter

You will carry your sadness, which will only add to your clutter

The Wilderness

Good morning everyone I hope you had a good sleep

Now today is a new Sunday, and this message won't keep

The bishop spoke about the wilderness of man

An expression so intense, we could no longer stand

He yelled, like always, to get his point across

Yet this morning he spoke about more than the cross

He spoke about how we are all led into the wilderness

Not knowing our next turn, not willing to confess

How long? he asked, will you wander around aimlessly?

Seeking your goal in a land not meant for you or me

How long will you wander, how long will you stray?

When all you need to do is kneel down and pray

The wilderness is large, for some it could last for years

How many are lost, how many of you feel God's tears?

If you believe in our Lord, then you should believe he'll bring you through

The Lord gave us grace; the Lord gave His son for you

So even when times are hard, even when you feel you can't make it

Look to the sky, because your steps are His script

So pick up your head and shake off your doubt

The wilderness leads to faith; I hope you know what I am talking about

Do It Again

Good afternoon everyone who lives a life of fear

Are you ready to move forward, or do you even care?

I am talking to those who still live in the past

Only looking at what happened, without getting a grasp

The bishop yelled "do it again. It's time to try again"

Have you learned from your enemy? The one you called your friend?

When you fall to the floor, do you stay down and weep?

Or do you stand up and look for that lonely creep?

You had a bad relationship, you had a bad time

Learn from what happened. A lesson isn't a crime

Your life isn't over because you suffered in your past

"Do it again", he yelled, because the pain won't last

How will you ever learn if you don't make a mistake?

The lesson isn't what happened, but what you've gained in its wake

"Do it again" he yelled, their life is a life you need to enjoy

Stop crying over your hurt and find yourself a new toy

So, your man or woman hurt you, and you seem to blame the world

How long will you complain about not finding a diamond or pearl?

Do it again means don't stop trying to find your heart

It will be a rough ride, are you ready for your new start?

Break The Rules

Wow. That's the word that expressed the message today

As we listened to the bishop on this warm, sunny day

This message spoke volumes to every single one of us

While our eyes filled with tears, nobody would dare fuss

He yelled "break the rules and your doors will open wide"

As he explained, with rules come walls that hold ideas inside

Like anything in life, they say rules are made to be broken

Yet, if you just sit back and accept life, then you become just another token

Some of us don't trust what the Lord has given to you and me

Now that is why we don't trust what others can clearly see

Haven't you ever noticed that until someone wants you, nobody else does?

Yet, once someone takes notice, their answer is yes, because

Sometimes you may have problems that may seem so out of reach

Yet, once you go to church, it is the message that was preached

While we don't feel how others see what's in our hearts

Some may be called handsome or pretty from the very start

You may feel fat or unworthy of a special woman or man

Yet, they still picked you for a reason that you don't understand

While you have low self-esteem, he or she has a different look

They have the spirit of Jesus who follows a different book

So remember, we all have beauty which we sometimes don't acknowledge

Just break the rules, because this message doesn't require college

Purpose Means Time

Today I heard a message that was so unique

It was one of substance that truly left me unable to speak

This message was delivered without any hesitation

As the bishop spoke, the Lord addressed our whole nation

You see, we all are placed on Earth to live out our fate

Now you have a purpose to complete before your expiration date

Too many of us waste away our God-given time

Not doing as instructed, now this should be a crime

Do you realize we are limited on the time we are given?

Are you here to serve your purpose, or just hoping to be forgiven?

When will you realize that with purpose we are given time?

Hopefully you will begin to value purpose, like you do every dime

There are several parallel walls that face you, here on Earth

Just like opposition and opportunity, who question what you're worth

Every time you've seen hope for something, and reached out to opportunity

Have you met Mr. Opposition, who has blocked what now cannot be?

That is why you must realize that your purpose means your time

Because if you expire without completing your purpose, that would be a crime

A Toxic Relationship

Well hi everyone, who has a special one in their life

Whether they're your lover, or a potential husband or a wife

I want you to take a look at that love you've found

Are they really what you need, or just fooling around?

Did you realize when you met that they carried a whip?

Always bringing drama, causing a toxic relationship

Do you have a person who is just an elevator ride?

Did they really want your loving, or was it just sex and pride?

Now, a relationship is like an elevator, it has its ups and downs

Have you found your future, or have you met Bozo the clown?

Look at what they've done with the time you've invested

Do you see yourself improving, or have your wits been tested?

I want you to question whether they are a refrigerator or a garbage can

Have they become one of trust, or someone you cannot stand?

We need to realize that your circle of friends should be small

Because in your time of need, will they answer your worried call?

So be careful who you trust, pay attention to their whip

Don't be fooled into having a toxic relationship

Lion Heart

Now I want you to understand her courage from the start

She is a strong little lady whose name should be Lion Heart

Now, her name is Trenaya, and she has a heart of gold

She has a heart of a lion, and that's the story that needs to be told

Now, many people know how to complain, but that isn't her style

She tells of her plans to leave her home town for a while

Now we are talking about a girl who was bright from the start

Bound from birth to a wheelchair, with a lion's heart

While most people would live in pity, and seek someone to blame

Not Trenaya. She grew her strength from her dad; never feeling any shame

You see, while her legs placed her in a wheelchair, this wasn't a curse

Only Trenaya could find a way to overcome the worst

She finished high school, and learned how to drive her own car

Not allowing life's obstacles to limit just how far

You see, Trenaya lost her dad, but she didn't lose her desire

While she misses his presence, she also keeps his fire

Trenaya now attends college, from Temple to the Florida Coast

Reaching for new heights, from a wheelchair, she gets the most

So, no matter what you're going through, remember Trenaya's shaky start

She still is a precious lady with her dad's Lion heart

The Real Question is Who Are You?

Good morning, my friends, I heard a new word today

This one was felt just like lingering tooth decay

Now I had to sit and ponder this message I heard

Because it had a powerful meaning for three simple words

The bishop yelled out his message, he yelled "who are you?"

He explained people I need you to look at yourself

Do you see God's perfection; do you see God's wealth?

When Jesus instructed his disciples to eat His bread at the table

He made them understand His words as they were able

When He instructed them to drink His blood which was wine

He explained how this would replace the Old Testament and everything would be fine

While the disciples ate and drank, as they heard His commands

The New Testament replaced the laws by the Lord's own hands

This meant that we must change our ways from old to new

A challenge indeed, because with change, fear grew

Yet the Lord reminds us that with faith there is no fear

Listen to my voice; it's all you should hear

Remember my words without doubting what to do

The real question is: Who are you?

The Lord Picked Me Up on the Highway

Today we heard a confession from a speaker named Dean

While he revealed his past today, he also revealed that he is clean

This stranger spoke about how he lived in a bottle, while he grew up

Little did he know how his life was about to erupt

Dean was run over by a car, while he laid drunk, in the street

While doctors gave him little hope, it was the Holy Spirit he would meet

The doctors told his parents they gave him little hope to survive

Yet the Lord had other plans to keep Dean alive

Dean grew up with a limp because damage to his body affected his spine

Until one day a stranger laid hands on him, and suddenly he was fine

Now, he and this friend took to the road with no destination in sight

Living for the moment, they just felt everything would be alright

Soon, his money ran out and his friend left him for a different path

Dean was all alone, unable to do the math

He was picked up by strangers, each one was sent by the Lord

While he didn't realize God's presence, they offered what he couldn't afford

Every time he took to the road, without a single dime

Along came a new stranger to offer God's word and time

Dean had become a believer; each turn became a road to the Lord

Each stranger who crossed his path told him to come on board

Today, Dean tells his story of how he became one of God's sheep

Proud to explain about how Jesus saved him from the Devil's keep

While he explained how Jesus makes our lives whole

It has become his mission to make sure his story is told

Need I Remind You?

Now I want you to listen to this message of today

Just pull up your own chair and pay attention to what I say

Now I know you have problems that may seem quite heavy

Yet instead of praying on it, you look at those you envy

Now I notice you complain about every other thing

Yet have you once looked at the problems that you bring?

Now I notice you call on the Lord to help, only when you need

So who is the selfish one, who is self-seeking their own greed?

Now let's look at what I've done for you, we'll only count today

Did you wake up this morning? Did you say thank you for this day?

Now let's look at what I've given you, without you even asking

I've given you your life, without asking for a thing

Now let's think about the blessings that you have received

Why do you go through life refusing to give praise or believe?

Now let's think about where you would be without my love

As I've watched over your life, while I lifted your spirit from above

Now think about your path, pay attention to what you do

And for those who seemed lost, I will ask "need I remind you?"

Ungrateful

Today I met a woman named Sherry

She was a beautiful lady whose life was a hurry

You see, this was a lady who was blessed to no end

Beauty and brains, with a life with God's friend

Yet the one thing she lacked was faith in the Holy Spirit

She stated I grew up in the Catholic church, but didn't want to hear it

Sherry spoke about how she grew up being poor

Saddened by her memory, as she looked to the floor

She spoke about how she spent her childhood in the hospital

Although she didn't enjoy her life, her spirit was full

As she grew older, she became a strong lady, indeed

While she enjoyed the Lord's blessings, so grew her greed

Now Sherry spoke about how she always helped without receiving

Giving off her back, yet she had no faith in what she was believing

She continued to speak about how God had let her down

This made me angry, and I could no longer hold my frown

How dare you complain about how God has treated you?

Did you ever review your life, as you live without a clue?

You come here for help, yet all you do is complain

Instead of looking at yourself, think about who caused your pain

God looked after you, picked you up and made you whole

Instead of giving thanks, you refuse to do as you are told

Why don't you stop and think of what life has given you?

Beauty and brains, yet you've been simply ungrateful

Great Faith In Thee

Today was a day that I learned a new meaning

Great faith in the Lord, as He allowed me to keep leaning

All throughout life we are challenged with grief

Yet if we have great faith, then we have His belief

We all receive a choice to listen to the word from Thee

Yet we second guess His word, now why should this be?

The Lord only asked that we give Him our praise

Instead we continue to second guess what He says

Come to me with your troubles, come with your fears

Once you humble your heart, I will erase your tears

When you learn to trust and believe in Thee

That will be the moment that your "I" changes to "we"

When the Lord spoke to you, He gave you a choice

Did you listen to His word? did you hear His voice?

From that moment, I felt the presence of Thee

It made me realize how He forgave a wretch like me

I Can't Complain

Today seemed like an ordinary day, indeed

While I walked on by, I only thought of my needs

The day was cloudy, when it started to rain

I saw a friend who yelled "I can't complain!"

Now, I had to think on this cloudy, cold day

Of all the comments, why he chose that phrase to say

So, I stopped and turned, and asked "what do you mean?"

He smiled at me and said "You think you're clean?"

So I asked, "Why would you ask me that question?"

He said "You should find Jesus, and that's not a suggestion.

When you realize the blessings that are given every day

Then you will understand the words that I say"

People of today are all Burger King babies

Treating each other like they have rabies

We all seem to want, but we are not willing to give

Why do so many hate, when they should forgive?

So, when I think about the man I met, in the rain

I now understand when he said "I can't complain!"

Fellas With a Second Chance

Today I met a man who had a story to tell

He spoke from his heart about the gates of hell

You see, while he gathered his thoughts, his eyes filled with tears

While he held them back, he spoke of his happiness, over the years

He spoke about his job that was dear to his heart

While he began to reminisce, it was hard for him to start

His job was a recruiter for a job that left most curious

Yet he gathered men from jail, who would take work very serious

So when he went to prison and informed them he would hire their newly released

Grateful for a second chance, those no longer needed to be policed

These men that he recruited became like a family to him

He didn't care about their past, whether they were Greg or Jim

These men were loyal, they worked hard every day

The only requirement was that they work hard and pray

His company lasted with them for over 23 years

When they decided to close down, it brought them to tears

He spoke of how he found the Lord while he asked "how could this be?"

You could feel his sadness, while he told his sad story

The Lord is Your Hope

Today's message was about the holy cross

It was about our Lord, who suffered the ultimate loss

How our lives were changed without us doing a thing

While the preacher spoke, it was the Holy Spirit he would bring

He asked could any of us do as Jesus did?

Could you give up your life, would you take that bid?

Our lives have been changed from that day till now

As we sit and think about it, our spirit says "wow"

The preacher spoke of how Jesus healed us from lost hope

He removed our sins from our neck, like a tightened rope

The preacher continued to speak of how we always live with pain

As we cry for relief, with our tears, God brings His rain

While we continue to live as part time Christians

Seeking the word, only when hard times need fixings

We are quick to defend, we are quick to protect and fight

Yet the question was asked; when will we start living right?

The word in the bible was issued from above

All Jesus did was deliver an unconditional love

So as you go through life, your cross may teach you how to cope

Look to the Lord, because the Lord is your hope

SHAWNA

Today I met a lady who wanted to tell her story

While she sat in my presence, she spoke of God's glory

Now this was a woman who seemed sad, for a moment

Yet what I didn't realize, was that her spirit was heaven sent

She spoke about a place that made her sadness fade

How she was lifted by the Lord, to a place heaven made

She spoke of how she had visited a place, not of this Earth

While she held back her tears, she felt her own worth

She said she was able to look down from the skies

Shawna watched, in amazement, with tears in her eyes

She said she saw all of her loved ones who had passed away

They were young and happy, on this amazing day

She saw fields of flowers and family and friends

Shawna spoke like a child, about her times way back when

She then felt her spirit starting to pull her away

While she begged to remain, a voice told her "not today"

Shawna spoke of how she felt her body fill with air

As she returned to our world, she was sad to return here

Now she lives her life without any fear of this world

Hoping to return to heaven as a blessed little girl

Palm Sunday

Good morning everyone, on this very blessed day

As we gather in church, it is to understand Palm Sunday

Nobody ever explained the meaning of the palms to me

How the Romans laid them down to symbolize their victory

Whenever their soldiers came back from a victory, of their fight

The palms were laid as a symbol, while the people danced all night

While we often wonder how this relates to the cross

It is because palms were laid down, before Jesus suffered His loss

Yet what they didn't realize, was that it wasn't a loss at all

Because when He was crucified, He made the ultimate call

So many of us go to church on Palm Sunday, without understanding

How Jesus took on the world's sins, which had become so demanding

Yet He loved us so much, and for this He carried the cross

Knowing the outcome, knowing what it would cost

So when we see those palms and we ponder what they mean

It is the Lord's victory for our grace, which had been foreseen

You don't read about the palms in the bible, because it was the Roman way

Yet we now have a different understanding about Palm Sunday

The Word is Our Water

Today I heard a message that was so powerful

It has a special meaning that for me, had no equal

The bishop spoke of how the word is like our water

While he explained his message, it was meant for every son and daughter

Like water to your body, your spirit needs the word

Now you may go through life thinking this message is absurd

In the bible you will find how the Lord loved Moses like a son

No matter what he did, the Lord blessed this holy one

The name Moses means taken from the water

He was ordained from birth, to lead every Jewish son and daughter

While he was taken from the water as a child, with a special deed

He was taken from his riches and placed with those in need

As Moses found out that our Lord had a task for him

While he asked Ramesses for freedom, the chances grew very slim

We must read the bible, it is the message for our soul

Like every hard headed person, we never do as we are told

The answers to our troubles are written in the word

Are you thirsty enough to remember what you've heard?

Heaven and Earth

Now I want you to think about what you are worth

Do you understand the true meaning of Heaven and Earth?

I want you to understand what is meant by family

Do you understand why the Lord looks after you and me?

Because like any family that sticks together, they remain strong

Yet you always find family members who feel like they don't belong

You have family members with you while you live here on Earth

Then there is our Father of the supernatural, who knows your true worth

Like a child who always comes to his father with a need

We are all God's children and He relies on our praise, not our greed

Do you realize your family is strong because of our Lord?

The Devil is a liar and he knows what he cannot afford

While we are here among the living, it's our goal to find our worth

Our Father guides our steps from the moment of our birth

Yet we often stray off and wander way off His course

Only to become confused, while our spirit becomes lost

So learn to call on your Father, because He knows your worth

While He sits on His throne and watches from Heaven over Earth

Obstacles

Good morning everyone who woke up with a problem

Did you think of a solution? Did you face any of them?

While you lay down to sleep, did you ever say thank you?

For living another day as God has continued to bless you?

When you look at a glass of water, is it half full?

Are you one who panics when your life hits an obstacle?

When the Lord puts a bump in your road, it is His test

Not for you to give up, He just doesn't want your mind to rest

When you are confronted on a path that you felt was yours

Are you ready for the challenge? Do you break down closed doors?

When you are given an obstacle, it is the Lord giving you a lesson

He wants you to become stronger, get ready for your next blessing

Why do you feel life should be easy, without any bumps?

This is how you become stronger, by taking your lumps

A person who never is challenged doesn't know of pain

Life brings you obstacles through which we must learn

So, tonight think about all the troubles you've been through

Because the results couldn't have come without having an obstacle!

Secret Anger

I want you to think about who you have become

Are you a person people seem to want to run from?

Have you lost your spirit, have you lost your own voice?

What once was a happy you, has been smothered with no choice

Do you hide your feelings to avoid a fight at home?

Let it out, or you will one day be all alone

People once loved your company, and called for your joy

Have you chased that spirit like a child with a broken toy?

How many people have built up themselves with secret anger?

Feeling like they must keep inside, as their vision becomes a blur

This secret anger is frustration, and it has made you change

The person with the joyful spirit has made a bad exchange

You've become a person who people want no part

Have your friends turned away, questioning your very start?

Take some time and pay attention to your kids

As they watch their parents fight, they're putting in their bids

These are all signs of your secret anger

Pay attention to the signs, because it's probably not her

I Hope You Understand

Good morning everyone who has awoken from their sleep

While you laid in your comfort, it was the Lord blessing His sheep

I would like you to pay attention to the fruit that you bear

Whether they are things you've requested, or blessings for you to share

We are all Gods fruit, and have a purpose on Earth

While you complain about life, the Lord cherishes your worth

I would like you to sit back and think about The Lord's request

There is not much more to life, than to give it your best

Each Sunday we go to church, to give praise to our King

Yet are you one who returns on Monday to do the same old things?

While we continue to sin,while our actions sometimes go astray

How many times did you give thanks? How often do you pray?

The reason I speak of the blessings from Thee

Is because I often ask why GOD has blessed a simple wretch like me.

None of us are perfect, yet we may act like we are

Yet we are created in His image, even if this hasn't taken us very far

While some may have plenty, yet others suffer without cause

When we ask for the reason, the answer came back just because

So I want you to be grateful for what you have been given

Not everyone appreciates the blessing of simply living

So, tonight just take a moment to reflect on what's at hand

Tomorrow isn't promised and I hope you understand

God's Position

Good morning everyone, I hope you understand

If you're within the sound of God's voice, then you are part of the plan

The sermon today was one that brought many to tears

While some are new believers, others have believed for many years

The message was about how the Lord places everyone in position

While we fight our own spirit, we challenge any opposition

Many of us are afraid of change or something new

Yet for God to bless others, He changes things around you

Not everyone will understand why things happen in their circle

While some see the glass half empty, others consider it half full

When you allow God to move you to a new position for exposure

You will then understand why He's moved your norm, and given you closure

God allows things to happen in your life, for His own reasons

Some things will be painful. That is the price for your new season

When you realize your blessings are only because you have been chosen

That is when you will finally hear the words that He has spoken

While things come to you, and others hate your success

They will never understand why you were chosen with nothing less

While you shine through every situation that seems impossible, to the opposition

That is because you've allowed God to get you ready for His position